W9-BGY-367

Making Memories

Written by Kim Kittle

Illustrated by Susan Simon

FAMILY CENTER OF WASH. CO.
684 S. [. . .]
West Bend WI 53095

Totline® Publications
A Division of Frank Schaffer Publications, Inc.
Torrance, California

*Dedicated to all the children whose lives
these ideas have touched over the years, and
to my three sons, for the inspiration they have
given me through their enthusiasm and love.*
Kim Kittle

Managing Editor: Mina McMullin
Editor: Durby Peterson
Contributing Editors: Kathleen Cubley, Jean Warren
Copyeditor: Kathy Zaun
Editorial Assistant: Mary Newmaster
Graphic Designer (Inside): Jill Kaufman
Graphic Designer (Cover): Brenda Mann Harrison
Production Manager: Janie Schmidt

©2000 by Totline® Publications. All rights reserved. Except for the
inclusion of brief quotations in a review, no part of this book may
be reproduced or utilized in any form or by any means, electronic
or mechanical, including photocopying, recording, or by any
information storage and retrieval system, without written
permission from the publisher.

ISBN: 1-57029-286-8

Printed in the United States of America
Published by Totline® Publications
23740 Hawthorne Blvd.
Torrance, CA 90505

Introduction

What can you easily make that can never be lost, but is worth more than all the treasures in the world? Memories of time spent with your child! With the gift of your company, you fill many important needs for your small child. Today's busy schedules make it too easy to let the day go by without giving our children what they need most: ourselves.

Making Memories is a collection of ideas for simple activities, crafts, and snacks that you and your child can enjoy at home. Tips, directions, and readily-available supplies are listed. As you look through your family's photo albums and relive the experiences, it will seem like only yesterday when you were engaged in these events. Life is so very short, and your child grows up so very fast!

Love and enjoy your children now, for the time you devote will last forever in their hearts. There is no substitute, and there is no second chance. The love is already there. Can you find the time?

A WORD ABOUT SAFETY—All the activities in this book are appropriate for young children. However, it is important that an adult supervise the activities to make sure that children do not put any materials or objects in their mouths. As for art materials, such as scissors, glue, or felt tip markers, use those that are specifically labeled as safe for children unless the materials are to be used only by an adult.

Contents

Celebrating Nature

Easy Art, Clever Crafts

Made You Think!

Remember That Special Day

Memory-Making Tips

1. The activities in this book are specially designed for an adult and child to do together. Get involved with your child and make it memorable!

2. Occasionally, invite your child's playmate or a grandparent to participate in the fun.

3. Each activity consists of two pages—an activity page and a reflection page. After completing the activity, be sure to take a moment to record your child's thoughts and words on the reflection page.

4. Use your own creativity to personalize each activity in ways that will make it more meaningful for you and your child.

5. Remember to date each project that you plan to keep.

6. If possible, have a camera close by. The memories are priceless!

7. Any time you work with paint or other messy materials, remember to protect your table and your child's clothing. Keep newspaper on hand—it works well. Also try letting your child wear an old adult-sized T-shirt over his or her own clothes.

My Self-Portrait

Celebrate your child's uniqueness with this simple activity.

You Will Need
- drawing paper
- markers or crayons
- mirror

Directions

1. Draw an oval on a sheet of paper. Try to make it the size of your child's face.

2. Give your child a handheld mirror or let her sit in front of a wall mirror.

3. Talk about her facial features and what they do. Invite her to draw her face in the oval using markers or crayons.

For More Fun
Do this activity every so often to record how your child's drawings progress and change through time.

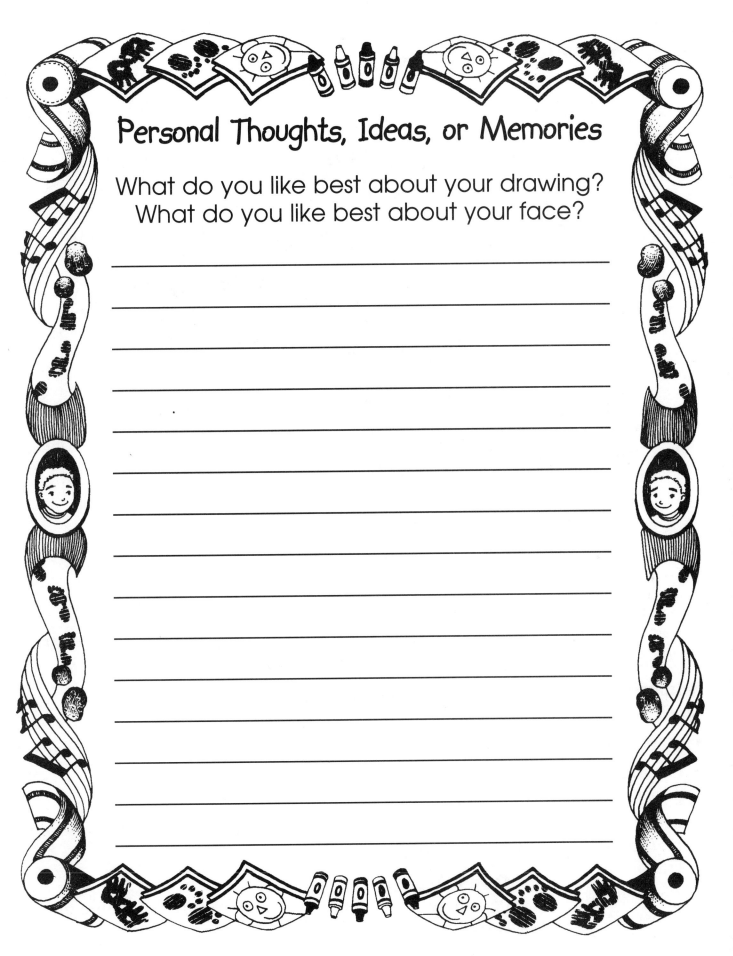

Personal Thoughts, Ideas, or Memories

What do you like best about your drawing?
What do you like best about your face?

_____

_____

_____

_____

_____

_____

_____

_____

_____

_____

_____

Handmade Placemat

This is the ideal gift for those faraway relatives.

You Will Need

- sponge
- paint
- construction paper or posterboard
- markers or crayons
- clear self-stick paper

Directions

1. Dip a sponge in paint and use it to coat both your child's hands with paint.

2. Let your child make handprints on construction paper or posterboard.

3. When the paint has dried (and his hands are clean), let him use markers or crayons to add to the placemat any designs he likes.

4. Cover the placemat with clear self-stick paper for durability.

Quick Tip

Remember to write the date and your child's name on this one!

Personal Thoughts, Ideas, or Memories

How does the paint feel on your hands?
What are some things you like to do
with your hands?

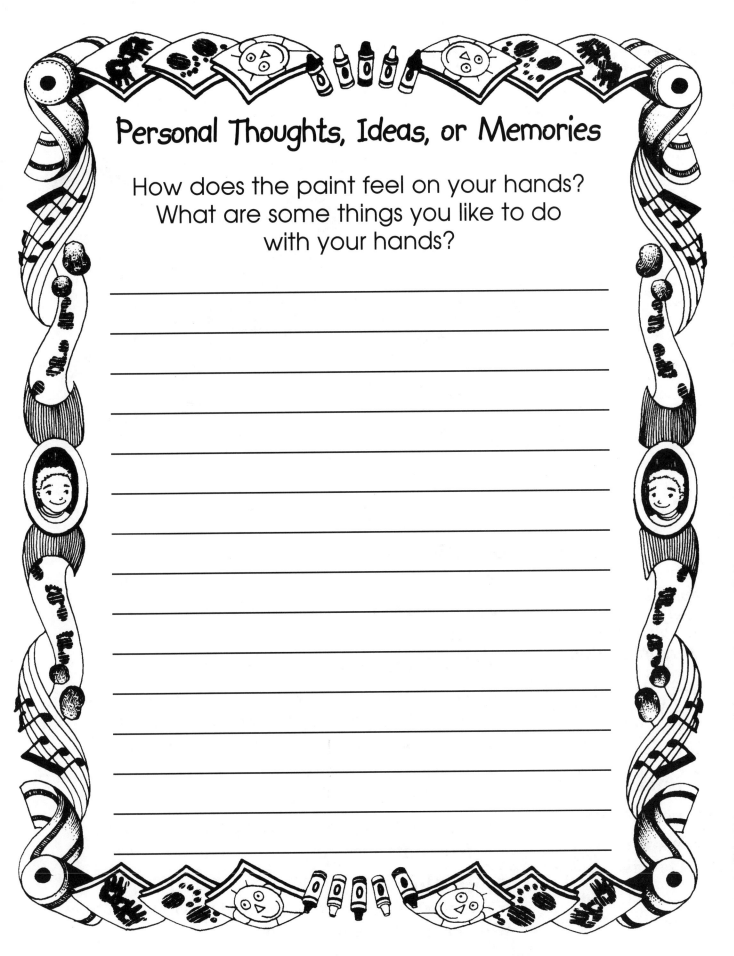

Footprints to Follow

Sept. 21, 1996 Sept. 15, 1997 Sept. 2, 1998 Aug. 26, 1999

Here is a keepsake that will let you tiptoe back to the past.

You Will Need
- tape
- 2 yards of white butcher paper
- sponge
- paint
- paper towels
- water

Directions
1. Tape 2 yards of butcher paper to the floor.
2. Using a sponge, coat the bottom of your child's foot with a thin layer of paint.
3. Press her foot on the paper to make a print.
4. Repeat the process with her other foot, making the second footprint slightly ahead of the first as if she were taking a step.
5. When dry, write the date near the footprints and put away the project until next year.
6. Each year, help your child make two new larger footprints ahead of the smaller ones.

Quick Tip
If too much paint is on your child's foot, lightly press with a paper towel to remove the excess.

Personal Thoughts, Ideas, or Memories

What do you want to be when you grow up? (Ask each year and see how the answers change!)

Dancing Feet

Let these potato "footprints" tickle your child!

You Will Need
- paint
- wide container, such as a baking pan
- masking tape
- large sheet of posterboard
- kitchen knife
- potato
- music

Directions
1. Put just enough paint in a container to cover the bottom.
2. Tape a sheet of posterboard onto a tabletop.
3. Halve a potato lengthwise so the cut part looks like an oval.
4. Show your child how to dip the potato into paint and blot it onto the posterboard.
5. Play some lively dancing music and invite your child to make dancing "footprints" all over the posterboard.
6. Have him add "toe" prints by dipping his thumb into the paint and making five little prints above each potato print.

For More Fun
Encourage your child to count the toes that he has painted on each "footprint."

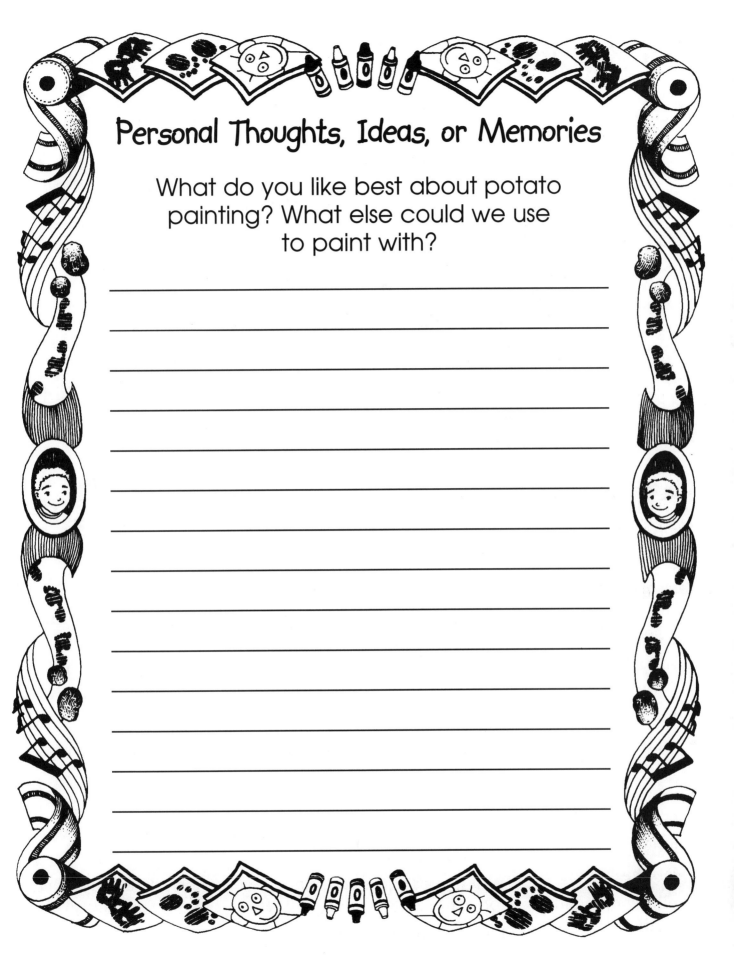

Personal Thoughts, Ideas, or Memories

What do you like best about potato painting? What else could we use to paint with?

_____

_____

_____

_____

_____

_____

_____

_____

_____

_____

_____

_____

_____

_____

_____

_____

I'm Building a House!

Your child will be thrilled with her little box house.

You Will Need
- appliance-size cardboard box
- craft knife or utility knife
- markers or crayons
- glue
- fabric scraps
- pillow or small chair

Directions

1. Prepare an appliance-size cardboard box by cutting out windows and a door.

2. Give your child markers or crayons and invite her to decorate both the inside and the outside of her box house.

3. Help her make real curtains by gluing fabric scraps to the tops of the windows.

4. Place a small pillow inside and let your child move in!

For More Fun

When cutting out the door, leave one vertical side uncut for a hinge. Your child will enjoy opening and closing her door.

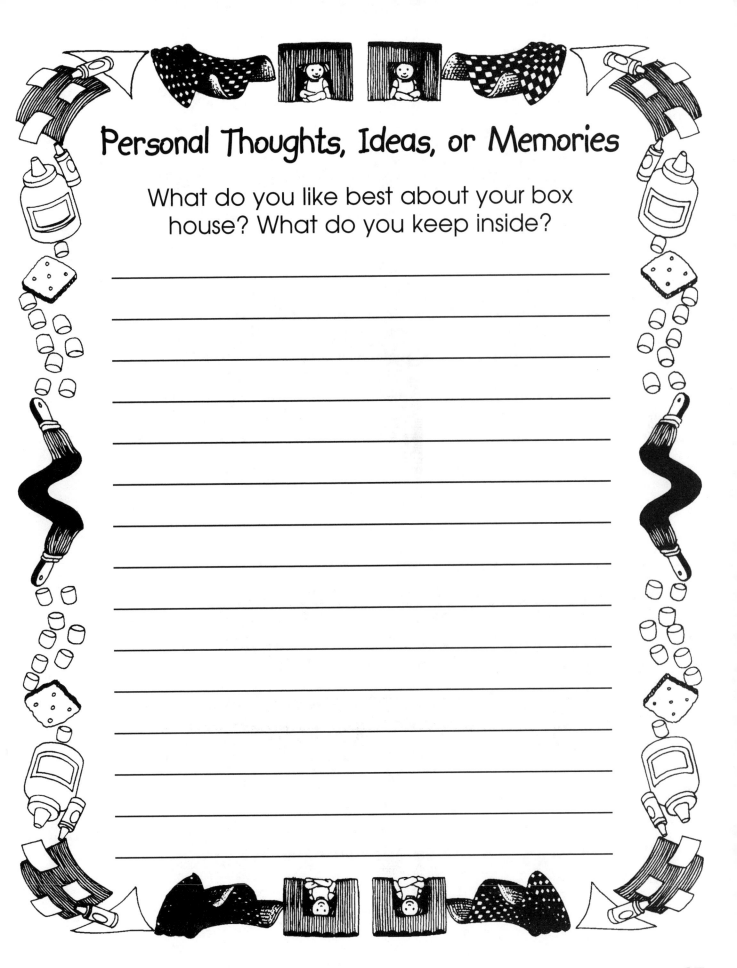

Personal Thoughts, Ideas, or Memories

What do you like best about your box house? What do you keep inside?

_____

_____

_____

_____

_____

_____

_____

_____

_____

_____

_____

_____

Home Sweet Home

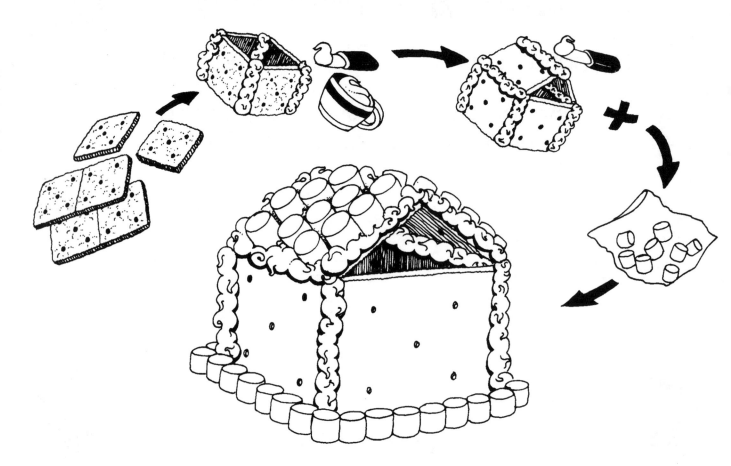

This childhood favorite tastes as yummy as it looks!

You Will Need

- 3 whole graham crackers
- 1 cup frosting
- food coloring (optional)
- plastic knife or wide craft stick
- small candies
- miniature marshmallows

Directions

1. Break three graham crackers in half to make six pieces.

2. Use frosting to bind four graham cracker halves together to form four walls.

3. With the two remaining halves, form an upside-down V-shaped roof and secure with frosting.

4. Give your child the remaining frosting (colored with food coloring, if desired), and let him paint his house with it.

5. Invite your child to decorate his house with small candies and marshmallows.

Quick Tip

Before using the frosting, refrigerate for three to six hours.

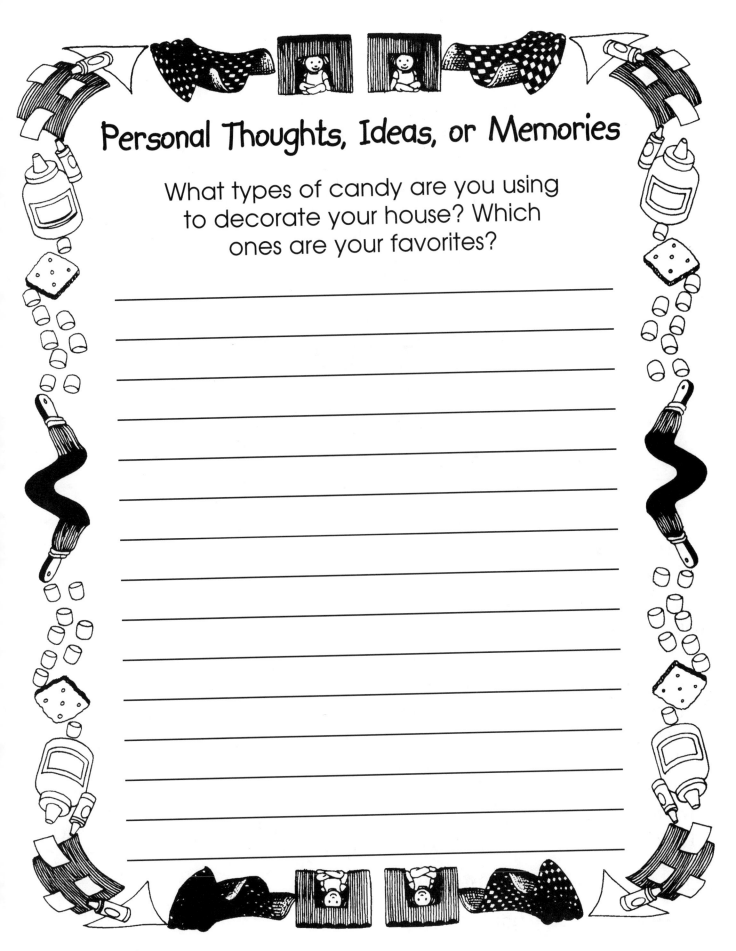

Personal Thoughts, Ideas, or Memories

What types of candy are you using
to decorate your house? Which
ones are your favorites?

_____

_____

_____

_____

_____

_____

_____

_____

_____

_____

_____

_____

_____

Shapes Under Construction

Give your child the tools to make this house take shape.

You Will Need

- construction paper in a variety of colors
- scissors
- white posterboard
- glue
- markers or crayons

Directions

1. Using construction paper in a variety of colors, cut out a large square, a triangle, a rectangle, and small squares for windows.

2. Give your child a piece of white posterboard and let her assemble the shapes on it to make a house.

3. Help her glue each piece into place.

4. Encourage your child to use markers or crayons to add some finishing touches around the house, such as flowers, grass, or a fence.

For More Fun

As your child works, take this opportunity to help her learn the basic shapes.

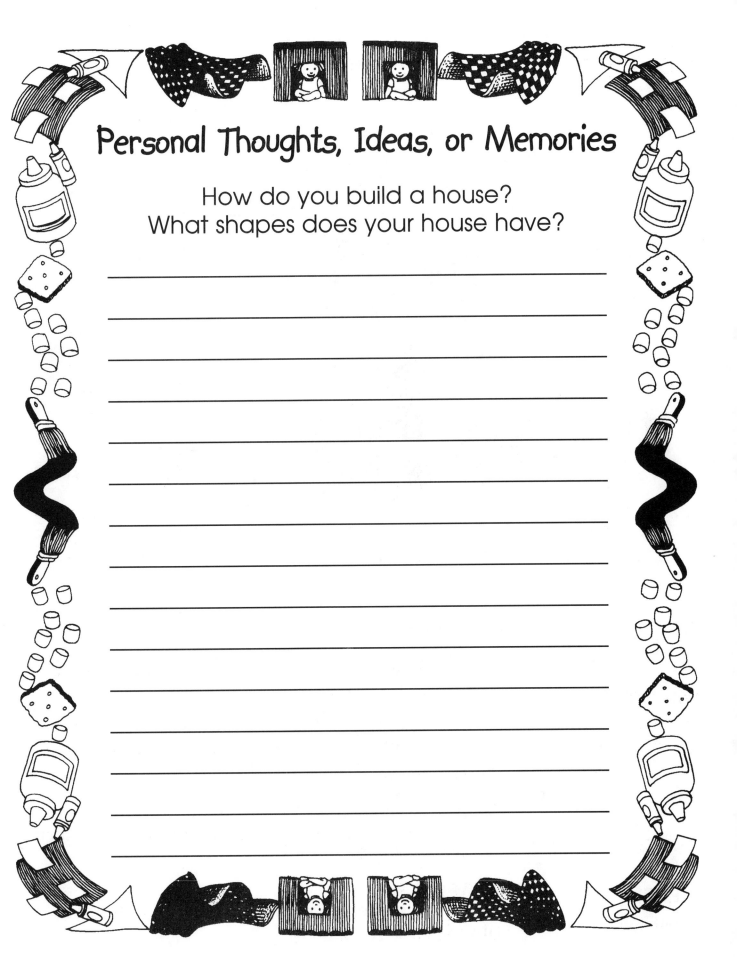

Personal Thoughts, Ideas, or Memories

How do you build a house?
What shapes does your house have?

_____

_____

_____

_____

_____

_____

_____

_____

_____

_____

_____

_____

Painter at Work

Watch how seriously your child takes this house-painting project!

You Will Need

- 3 feet of butcher paper
- marker
- tape
- newspaper
- paint
- large paintbrush

Directions

1. On butcher paper, draw a basic house shape, at least two feet tall, with a roof.

2. Tape the drawing onto a solid structure, such as a wall or backyard fence.

3. Spread newspaper below to catch any paint drippings.

4. Let your child paint his house.

5. Leave hanging until dry.

For More Fun

As your child works, encourage him to tell you about various rooms of his house.

Personal Thoughts, Ideas, or Memories

What color is your house? Which part is the most fun to paint? Why?

_____

_____

_____

_____

_____

_____

_____

_____

_____

_____

_____

_____

My Name Is Crunchy!

Here is a clever way to show your child the spelling of her name.

You Will Need
- pencil
- white construction paper
- small bits of food

Directions

1. Print your child's name in large letters on a piece of white construction paper. (If your child can write her name, let her do the printing.)

2. Set out small bits of food, such as miniature marshmallows, chocolate chips, popcorn, or cereal, and invite your child to place them on the letters of her name.

3. Let her eat the goodies when she is done!

For More Fun
Your child will enjoy hearing how you selected her name. Does it have a special meaning? Was she named after a loved one?

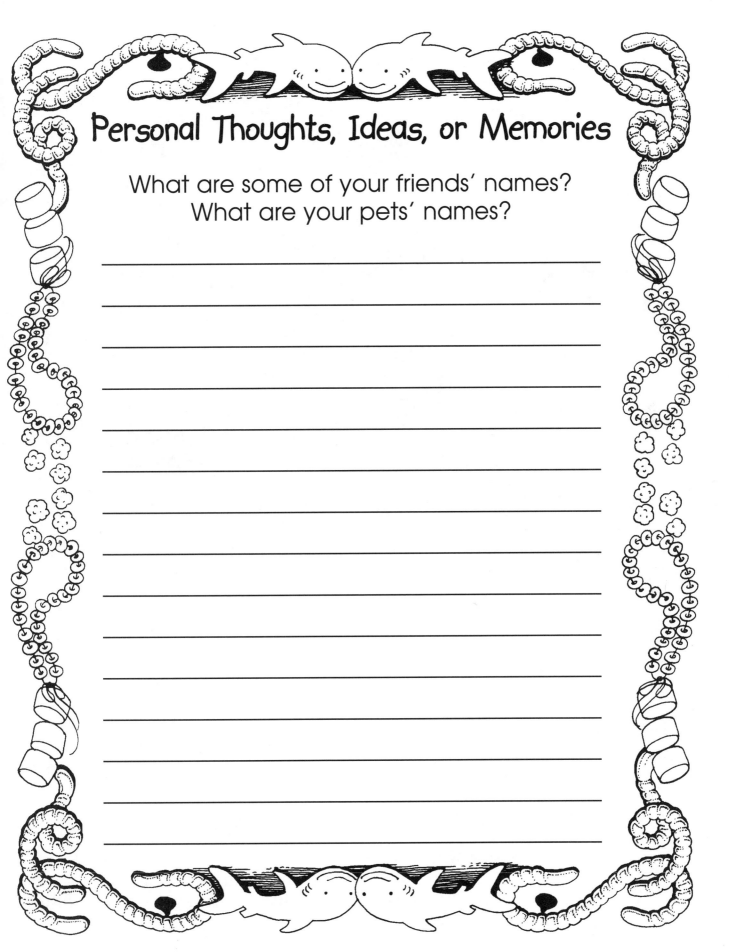

Personal Thoughts, Ideas, or Memories

What are some of your friends' names?
What are your pets' names?

Delicious Dirt

How can something that looks like dirt taste delicious?

You Will Need
- chocolate cookies
- large resealable plastic bag
- rolling pin
- clear plastic cups
- chocolate ice cream or pudding
- chewy candy worms
- spoons

Directions
1. Place about 12 chocolate cookies inside a plastic bag and seal.

2. Help your child use a rolling pin to crush the cookies into fine crumbs.

3. Fill several clear plastic cups about half full with either chocolate ice cream or pudding.

4. Place a chewy candy worm on top of the chocolate so it is visible from the side.

5. Add crushed cookie crumbs to fill the cup.

Quick Tip
Let your child help you make this treat, or you may have trouble convincing him that it is really food and not dirt!

Personal Thoughts, Ideas, or Memories

What else could we sprinkle on top of the worm? Do you think this treat looks like dirt? How does it taste?

_____

_____

_____

_____

_____

_____

_____

_____

_____

_____

_____

_____

_____

_____

Scrumptious Snowman

This adorable little snowman is sure to be a treat!

You Will Need
- white frosting
- 3 large marshmallows
- raisins
- chocolate chips
- pretzel sticks
- coconut

Directions
1. Use frosting to stick together three large marshmallows, one on top of another.
2. Add raisins and chocolate chips to make eyes and a mouth.
3. Break off a small piece of pretzel for a nose.
4. Use long pretzel sticks to make twig arms.
5. Sprinkle shredded coconut around the snowman to resemble snow.

For More Fun
Sing or play a recording of "Frosty the Snowman" and let your child make her snowman dance around.

Personal Thoughts, Ideas, or Memories

Does your little snowman have a name?
What should we do the next time it snows?

_____

_____

_____

_____

_____

_____

_____

_____

_____

_____

_____

_____

_____

_____

_____

Nibble a Necklace

Try this decorative and delicious idea on for size!

You Will Need
- O-shaped cereal or candy
- bag or bowl
- 3 feet of string or yarn

Directions

1. Give your child a supply of O-shaped cereal or candy in a bowl or bag.

2. Tie one piece of O-shaped cereal or candy to the end of a 3-foot piece of string.

3. Show your child how to string the cereal or candy, one piece at a time, onto the necklace.

4. When he is finished, tie the ends together.

5. Let your child wear (and nibble on) his hand-crafted necklace.

Quick Tip
This is a great way to help your child develop coordination skills. Extend the learning by helping him count the items on his necklace.

Personal Thoughts, Ideas, or Memories

Which is more fun, making a necklace or eating it? Why?

_____

_____

_____

_____

_____

_____

_____

_____

_____

_____

_____

_____

_____

Play With Your Pudding!

There's nothing like a pile of pudding for hands-on fun!

You Will Need
- 3 feet of wax paper
- tape
- chocolate pudding

Directions
1. Spread wax paper onto a table.
2. Secure with tape.
3. Have your child wash her hands well before beginning this project.
4. Place a large scoop of chocolate pudding on the wax paper.
5. Invite your child to use the pudding as fingerpaint and make designs with it all around the paper.
6. Afterward, enjoy a bowl of pudding together!

Quick Tip
This activity is great for breaking the ice when your child invites over a new friend.

Personal Thoughts, Ideas, or Memories

How does it feel to have pudding all over your hands? How do you clean them off?

_____

_____

_____

_____

_____

_____

_____

_____

_____

_____

_____

_____

_____

Funny Fish

Make a snack that appeals to your child's appetite and imagination.

You Will Need
- blue packaged gelatin (wild berry flavor)
- gummy candy fish or sharks

Directions

1. Prepare blue (berry-flavored) gelatin as the package directs.

2. When the gelatin begins to firm, let your child add gummy fish or sharks.

3. When the snack has completely jelled, serve it for your child to enjoy.

For More Fun
Prepare the snack in several small clear bowls so they look like fishbowls. Let your child count the fish as he drops them into each bowl.

Personal Thoughts, Ideas, or Memories

What do fish like to do? Do you think it would be fun to be a fish?

_____

_____

_____

_____

_____

_____

_____

_____

_____

_____

_____

_____

_____

_____

Pack Your Suitcase

Watch all the fun that a suitcase can pack into your child's day!

You Will Need
- construction paper
- scissors
- tape
- magazine pictures
- glue

Directions

1. Fold in half a large piece of construction paper.

2. Cut construction-paper suitcase handles and attach with tape.

3. Give your child magazine pictures of items she might take on a trip.

4. Open the suitcase and let her select pictures to glue inside.

For More Fun

As your child carries her completed suitcase around, give her additional traveling props, such as dress-up clothes and pretend tickets. She will love the adventure!

Personal Thoughts, Ideas, or Memories

What do you keep in your suitcase?
What are some places you would like
to travel to? How would we get there?

_____
_____
_____
_____
_____
_____
_____
_____
_____
_____
_____
_____
_____
_____
_____

Green Is for Go!

With this prop, your child is on the road to adventure!

You Will Need

- scissors
- construction paper
- round object, such as a soup can
- pencil
- glue
- ruler

Directions

1. Cut from black construction paper an 18-by-6-inch rectangle.

2. Using a round object, trace one circle each on red, green, and yellow construction paper.

3. Help your child cut out the circles.

4. Let your child glue the circles onto the rectangle with red on top, yellow in the middle, and green on the bottom.

5. When finished, talk with your child about what the colors mean in traffic.

For More Fun

Tape the traffic signal to your child's bedroom door and ask him if the light is green so you can enter!

Personal Thoughts, Ideas, or Memories

What kind of car would you like to drive?
What would you do when the light
turned green? Where would you go?

_____

_____

_____

_____

_____

_____

_____

_____

_____

_____

_____

_____

_____

Stop at the Sign

Your child will direct traffic all over the house!

You Will Need
- red paint
- paper plate
- child's paintbrush
- scissors
- white construction paper
- glue
- wide craft stick

Directions
1. Have your child paint an entire paper plate bright red.
2. Cut capital letters from white construction paper to spell the word STOP.
3. Help your child glue the letters onto the (dried) paper plate.
4. Glue a craft stick onto the bottom of the plate to use as a handle.

Quick Tip
Your child will stop you again and again with this sign. Be prepared for a stop-and-go day!

Personal Thoughts, Ideas, or Memories

Why do we need stop signs on the roads?
What other things do you see as we ride
around town?

_____

_____

_____

_____

_____

_____

_____

_____

_____

_____

_____

_____

_____

_____

_____

Sidewalk City

Join in for an afternoon of fun and watch your child at play!

You Will Need
- safe sidewalk area
- large boxes
- toys, snacks, or other props
- trike or wagon

Directions

1. Find a safe sidewalk area that provides plenty of room.

2. Use large boxes to create pretend businesses along the way, such as a favorite restaurant, a pet store, or a library.

3. Include simple props, such as snacks at the restaurant, stuffed animals at the pet store, and a basket for returning books at the library.

4. Encourage your child to use his trike or wagon along your pretend street.

Quick Tip
Get involved as the librarian or storekeeper and help your child bring this town to life!

Personal Thoughts, Ideas, or Memories

What is your favorite restaurant? If you had
your own business, what would it be?

_____

_____

_____

_____

_____

_____

_____

_____

_____

_____

_____

_____

_____

My Magnifying Glass

You and your child will enjoy taking a close look at nature.

You Will Need
- magnifying glass

Directions

1. Give your child a magnifying glass and let her discover how it works.

2. Take a nature walk with your child and encourage her to notice the details in seeds, flowers, and grass.

3. Collect a few of her favorite nature items and bring them inside to place on a "nature table" along with the magnifying glass.

4. Periodically, add to your collection other interesting nature items for your child to examine, such as shells, leaves, or pine cones.

For More Fun

Create a pretend magnifying glass by hot gluing a craft stick handle onto a clear yogurt lid. Your child's imagination will do the rest.

Personal Thoughts, Ideas, or Memories

What was the smallest thing you found on our walk? What was the most interesting thing you found?

_____

_____

_____

_____

_____

_____

_____

_____

_____

_____

_____

_____

_____

Little Tree for Me

Watch your child's creativity branch out in all directions!

You Will Need
- leaves collected on a nature walk
- scissors
- brown construction paper
- glue
- white posterboard
- markers or crayons

Directions

1. Take a nature walk with your child and collect a variety of leaves.

2. Cut out of brown construction paper a tree trunk.

3. Have your child glue the trunk onto white posterboard.

4. Let him glue the leaves on the posterboard wherever he chooses.

5. Give him markers or crayons to add other nature items, such as bugs and flowers.

Quick Tip
If no leaves are available, have your child tear green, yellow, orange, and red construction paper into "leaves."

Personal Thoughts, Ideas, or Memories

What colors are the leaves you found?
Where did you find them? Where
would like to put your little tree?

_____

_____

_____

_____

_____

_____

_____

_____

_____

_____

_____

_____

_____

_____

_____

Finger Flowers

This is one piece of artwork you will want to frame and display!

You Will Need
- white construction paper
- paint (green and a variety of other bright colors)
- sponge
- water

Directions
1. Set out white paper on a table.
2. Sponge green paint on one side of your child's arm.
3. Have your child stamp her arm on the paper to make a stem.
4. Repeat the process to make as many stems as you wish.
5. Sponge green paint onto the side of your child's hand and have her stamp it on the paper to make leaf prints on each stem.
6. Sponge various bright colors of paint onto your child's palm and fingers to make flower prints above the stems.
7. Let dry and hang or frame.

For More Fun
Make a custom border for your child's room by printing finger flowers on a long roll of butcher paper.

Personal Thoughts, Ideas, or Memories

What did you like best about making sponge flowers? What colors are the petals?

_____

_____

_____

_____

_____

_____

_____

_____

_____

_____

_____

_____

_____

A Special Sunflower

Something about a sunflower always brings a smile.

You Will Need

- paper plate
- yellow marker or crayon
- scissors
- yellow tissue or crepe paper
- glue
- unshelled sunflower seeds
- ruler

Directions

1. Give your child a paper plate and have him color it yellow.

2. Cut yellow tissue paper or crepe paper into 10 strips about 12 inches long.

3. Have your child glue the strips around the edge of the plate so that they extend outward to look like petals.

4. Spread some glue in the center of the plate.

5. Let your child glue unshelled sunflower seeds all over the center.

For More Fun

Share with your child a snack of sunflower seeds as you talk about the interesting flower that produces them.

Personal Thoughts, Ideas, or Memories

How many seeds do you think a sunflower has?
What makes the seeds stick to real sunflowers?

_____

_____

_____

_____

_____

_____

_____

_____

_____

_____

_____

_____

_____

Sunshine!

Here is a cheery idea, sure to brighten your child's day.

You Will Need
- scissors
- yellow construction paper
- ruler
- glue
- marker or crayon (optional)

Directions
1. Cut an 8-inch circle from yellow construction paper.
2. Cut yellow construction paper into eight 1-by-5-inch strips.
3. Have your child glue the yellow strips onto the back of the circle so that they extend beyond the edges like sun rays.
4. When dry, hang the paper sun in your child's window.

Quick Tip
Let your child do as much of this project as she can, such as cutting the strips. She might enjoy using a marker to add some eyes and a smiling mouth.

Personal Thoughts, Ideas, or Memories

Where will you hang your paper sun?
What do you like to do on sunny days?

_____

_____

_____

_____

_____

_____

_____

_____

_____

_____

_____

_____

_____

Terrific Tissue Flowers

Your child will be delighted with the way these colors collide!

You Will Need

- scissors
- brightly-colored tissue paper (including green)
- small bowl
- glue
- water
- white construction paper
- paintbrush
- ruler

Directions

1. Cut green tissue paper into 1-inch-wide strips to resemble flower stems.

2. Cut brightly-colored tissue paper into 1-inch squares.

3. In a small bowl, mix one part glue with one part water.

4. Give your child a piece of white construction paper and let him use a paintbrush to spread the glue mixture all over the paper.

5. Help him place green tissue paper strips on the paper.

6. Have your child add tissue squares to the top of the stems to form blossoms.

7. Help him paint more glue mixture onto the stems and blossoms.

Quick Tip

Help your child paint until the tissue paper is completely covered, but not soaked.

Personal Thoughts, Ideas, or Memories

Did anything surprise you about this project? What was the most fun about making these flowers?

_____

_____

_____

_____

_____

_____

_____

_____

_____

_____

_____

_____

_____

Rice Looks Nice

Here is a great kitchen project for rainy day fun.

You Will Need
- small bowls
- measuring cup
- uncooked rice
- food coloring
- spoon
- marker or crayon
- white construction paper
- paintbrush
- glue

Directions

1. Set out several small bowls.

2. Help your child scoop ¼ cup uncooked rice into each bowl.

3. Add a few drops of food coloring to each bowl.

4. Let your child use a spoon to mix in the color.

5. While the rice is drying, have your child draw a design on white paper.

6. Help her paint one area with glue.

7. Let her sprinkle rice onto the area she painted and shake off the excess.

8. Repeat the process with more glue and other colors of rice.

Quick Tip
Save any leftover colored rice in resealable plastic bags for another day's project.

Personal Thoughts, Ideas, or Memories

What kind of picture did you make?
How many colors did you use?

_____

_____

_____

_____

_____

_____

_____

_____

_____

_____

_____

_____

_____

Fun With Frames

Your child will take pride in this handcrafted frame.

You Will Need
- craft sticks
- glue
- small decorations
- scissors
- picture

Directions
1. Place four craft sticks in a rectangular design, overlapping at the corners.

2. Help your child glue the sticks together at the corners.

3. Spread glue onto the front of the stick frame.

4. Let your child place small decorations, such as beads, sequins, dyed macaroni, or shells, on the glue.

5. Cut a favorite picture to fit and then glue it to the back of the frame.

For More Fun
This project makes a great gift for a relative or friend.

Personal Thoughts, Ideas, or Memories

Who did you make your frame for?
What is special about this person?

_____

_____

_____

_____

_____

_____

_____

_____

_____

_____

_____

_____

_____

_____

_____

Ice Cream Colors

Here is some artwork that looks yummy enough to eat!

You Will Need

- scissors
- brown corrugated cardboard
- glue
- white posterboard
- construction paper in various colors
- colored rice or glitter (optional)

Directions

1. Cut from cardboard a long, narrow triangle.

2. Let your child glue the triangle onto white posterboard.

3. Cut colorful construction paper into circles the size of ice cream scoops.

4. Have your child glue above the cardboard cone as many paper circles as she wants.

5. If desired, let your child spread glue and sprinkle colored rice or glitter on the paper circles to resemble candy sprinkles.

6. When dry, hang up as a wall decoration.

For More Fun

This activity is sure to inspire a craving, so be prepared to serve real ice cream cones afterward!

Personal Thoughts, Ideas, or Memories

How many scoops did you put on your
paper cone? What is your favorite
flavor of ice cream?

_____

_____

_____

_____

_____

_____

_____

_____

_____

_____

_____

_____

_____

Objects of Art

Watch your child become absorbed in this activity!

You Will Need

- white construction paper
- paint
- small containers
- various washable household objects

Directions

1. Give your child a large piece of white construction paper.

2. Place a few different colors of paint in separate containers.

3. Set out at least six small objects for your child to choose from, such as forks, cookie cutters, soup cans, or bottle caps.

4. Invite your child to dip each object in the paint and press it onto the paper.

5. Encourage him to make as many prints as he wants, observing the different marks he creates.

Quick Tip

For best results, try to find objects in an interesting variety of shapes, sizes, and textures.

Personal Thoughts, Ideas, or Memories

What did you use to make your picture?
What else could we use to make prints?

_____

_____

_____

_____

_____

_____

_____

_____

_____

_____

_____

_____

_____

It's a Dinosaur!

This giant creature is sure to capture your child's imagination!

You Will Need

- 8 feet of white butcher paper
- black marker
- sponge
- paint
- scissors
- stapler
- newspaper

Directions

1. Fold an 8-foot section of butcher paper in half lengthwise and draw a dinosaur on one side.

2. Use the first drawing as a pattern to trace another dinosaur on the back of the fold.

3. Open up the paper onto a table so that both drawings are visible.

4. Invite your child to dip a sponge into some paint and blot it onto both dinosaur drawings.

5. When dry, cut out the dinosaurs and staple together, leaving a 2-foot opening.

6. Let your child stuff crumpled newspaper inside.

7. Staple the opening shut and hang it up to display.

Quick Tip

For drawing help, look in a picture book that features simplified dinosaur drawings and copy the lines. Your child will be delighted with the result!

Personal Thoughts, Ideas, or Memories

Does your dinosaur have a name?
What does your dinosaur like to do?

_____

_____

_____

_____

_____

_____

_____

_____

_____

_____

_____

_____

_____

_____

_____

Watermelon Slice

This idea brings more smiles than a watermelon has seeds!

You Will Need

- scissors
- paper plate
- red and green markers
- glue
- watermelon seeds

Directions

1. Cut a paper plate in half.

2. Use a green marker to section off the outer rim.

3. Have your child color the rim green to make the rind.

4. Invite her to color the fruit part of the watermelon red.

5. Help your child put small dots of glue on the red area.

6. Let your child glue on watermelon seeds.

Quick Tip

If you don't have watermelon seeds, use a hole punch to create "seeds" from black construction paper. Help your child count all the seeds!

Personal Thoughts, Ideas, or Memories

How many seeds are on your watermelon?
What do you like best about watermelon?

_____

_____

_____

_____

_____

_____

_____

_____

_____

_____

_____

_____

_____

_____

What's in the Box?

Keep this box handy and play the game over and over again!

You Will Need

- shoebox
- construction paper
- tape or glue
- markers or crayons
- scissors
- a small, familiar household item

Directions

1. Cover a shoebox with construction paper.
2. Let your child decorate the box with markers or crayons.
3. Add some question marks on the outside of the box.
4. Without letting your child see, place inside the box a small item from around the house that your child can identify by sight.
5. Lift the lid just enough so that your child can slip her hand inside.
6. Let your child feel around inside the box and try to identify the object.
7. Change the object and begin the game again.

For More Fun

Have your child find objects to place in the box for you to identify!

Personal Thoughts, Ideas, or Memories

How did you know what was in the box?
What else would fit inside the box?

_____
_____
_____
_____
_____
_____
_____
_____
_____
_____
_____
_____
_____
_____

Graphs Are Great!

Anything goes on this easy-to-make graph!

You Will Need
- marker
- construction paper
- glue
- 15 small objects

Directions

1. Draw four vertical lines on a piece of construction paper to divide it into five sections.

2. Write the numerals 1 through 5 across the top to number the sections.

3. Set out glue and 15 small objects, such as bottle caps, old stamps, paper clips, raisins, cereal bits, stickers, etc.

4. Invite your child to look at the number at the top of each section and then glue the corresponding number of objects down below.

For More Fun
After your child masters this challenge, encourage him to place one type of object in each column, such as one bottle cap, two stamps, three paper clips, etc.

Personal Thoughts, Ideas, or Memories

What are some of the things on your graph?
What else could we use for making graphs?

_____

_____

_____

_____

_____

_____

_____

_____

_____

_____

_____

_____

_____

_____

Shape Match-Up

This simple puzzle comes in all shapes and sizes!

You Will Need
- objects in various shapes
- marker
- construction paper

Directions

1. Collect a variety of small objects in a variety of shapes, such as round soup cans, square tissue paper boxes, or star-shaped cookie cutters.

2. Trace all the objects onto a single piece of large construction paper.

3. Invite your child to select one object at a time and find its matching shape on the paper.

4. When your child masters this puzzle, increase the challenge by using similar objects in different sizes, such as small, medium, and large blocks.

For More Fun
Cut various shapes out of colorful index cards, trace them onto paper, and let your child glue them onto the correct drawings.

Personal Thoughts, Ideas, or Memories

What shapes did you match?
Which ones are your favorites?

_____

_____

_____

_____

_____

_____

_____

_____

_____

_____

_____

_____

_____

FAMILY CENTER OF WASH. CO.
684 S. Indiana Ave
West Bend WI 53095

My Little Book

Your child will be delighted to make his own little book!

You Will Need
- scissors
- construction paper in assorted colors
- ruler
- glue
- stapler

Directions
1. Cut several pieces of construction paper into 5-inch-square book pages.
2. Set out some pre-cut shapes and glue.
3. Invite your child to glue a pre-cut shape onto each page.
4. Print the name of the shape at the bottom of each page.
5. Staple the pages together to create a book.
6. Print a title such as "Justin's Shape Book" on the front.

For More Fun
Help your child make a series of books to show different shapes and colors. Possibilities include "My Red Shape Book," "My Blue Shape Book," "My Colorful Triangle Book," "My Colorful Square Book," etc.

Personal Thoughts, Ideas, or Memories

What was the most fun thing about
making your book? Who would you
like to read your book to?

_____

_____

_____

_____

_____

_____

_____

_____

_____

_____

_____

_____

Touch a Texture

Stimulate your child's senses with a book that feels fun!

You Will Need

- household items with unique textures
- scissors
- construction paper
- ruler
- glue
- stapler
- marker

Directions

1. Collect a variety of household items with unique textures, such as sandpaper, cotton balls, sponges, tissue paper, and aluminum foil.

2. Count your texture items and cut from construction paper the same number of 5-inch squares.

3. Have your child glue one texture item onto each square.

4. Staple the squares together to make a small book.

5. Print your child's name on the front of the book.

Quick Tip

If your child can write, let her print her name on the book.

Personal Thoughts, Ideas, or Memories

What do you have in your book?
Is there something that feels bumpy?
Smooth? Slippery?

_____

_____

_____

_____

_____

_____

_____

_____

_____

_____

_____

_____

Centipede Count

This friendly creature will help your child learn different colors.

You Will Need
- markers
- 2-inch circle shape, such as a small jar lid
- construction paper
- scissors
- tape
- glue
- toothpicks

Directions

1. Use a marker to trace ten 2-inch circles on colored construction paper.

2. If your child can use scissors, let him cut out the circles.

3. Number the circles 1 through 10.

4. Encourage your child to put the circles in numerical order to form a centipede.

5. Help your child tape the circles together.

6. Let your child add a face to circle number 1.

7. Help your child glue on toothpicks to make legs.

Quick Tip
If you wish, make the circles out of different colors to help your child learn his colors.

Personal Thoughts, Ideas, or Memories

Can you think of a name for your centipede?
What else could we make out of circles?

_____

_____

_____

_____

_____

_____

_____

_____

_____

_____

_____

_____

Hot or Cold?

Here is an activity that will really make your child think!

You Will Need

- scissors
- magazine pictures of items that are hot and cold
- marker
- construction paper
- glue

Directions

1. Cut from magazines an assortment of pictures featuring things that are either hot or cold, such as ice cream, coffee, a toaster, or ski slopes.

2. Use a marker to divide a large piece of construction paper in half.

3. Give your child the pictures and talk about different things that are hot and cold.

4. Have your child glue pictures of hot items on one side of the paper and cold items on the other.

Quick Tip

If magazine pictures are not available, just draw simple pictures with your child.

Personal Thoughts, Ideas, or Memories

What are some cold things on your paper?
What are some hot things?
Which ones do you like best?

_____

_____

_____

_____

_____

_____

_____

_____

_____

_____

_____

_____

Gone Fishin'

Your child will want to play with this fishing pole again and again!

You Will Need

- pencil
- construction paper
- scissors
- paper clips
- kite string
- 3-foot wooden dowel (or thin stick)
- donut-shaped magnet, about ¾-inch in diameter

Directions

1. Draw simple fish shapes in small, medium, and large sizes on construction paper.

2. Cut out each fish.

3. Place a paper clip on each fish cutout.

4. Tie kite string to the end of a wooden dowel.

5. Attach a small donut-shaped magnet to the free end of the string for the "hook."

6. Give your child the homemade fishing pole and let him go fishing.

For More Fun

Write numbers, letters, or draw with different colors on the fish cutouts and let your child fish for different things.

Personal Thoughts, Ideas, or Memories

How many fish did you catch? Would you like to go on a real fishing trip? Where would you like to go?

_____

_____

_____

_____

_____

_____

_____

_____

_____

_____

_____

_____

_____

_____

Now That's a Hat!

Here's a hat that will fit just about any celebration.

You Will Need
- scissors
- construction paper
- glue
- assorted decorations
- tape
- ruler

Directions

1. Cut from construction paper a 3-inch-wide band, long enough to fit around your child's head.

2. Set out glue and assorted decorations, such as glitter, sequins, pipe cleaners, stickers, markers, and crayons.

3. Invite your child to add decorations to the construction paper hat to celebrate holidays, birthdays, or any special day.

4. Tape the ends together securely and let your child don her new hat!

Quick Tip
Keep a collection of miscellaneous supplies on hand to make your hats even more elaborate. You might collect things such as feathers, streamers, old greeting card pictures, etc.

Personal Thoughts, Ideas, or Memories

What did you put on your hat?
What is your favorite special day?

_____

_____

_____

_____

_____

_____

_____

_____

_____

_____

_____

_____

_____

_____

Happy Heart Necklace

Your day will be a little sweeter with this Valentine's Day necklace!

You Will Need
- scissors
- red construction paper
- hole punch
- kitchen knife
- red licorice twists
- 3 feet of string
- ruler

Directions
1. Cut out of red construction paper about ten 2-inch hearts.
2. Punch a hole in the center of each heart.
3. Cut red licorice into 1-inch lengths.
4. Tie one piece of licorice to the end of a string to keep the decorations from sliding off.
5. Let your child string licorice and paper hearts alternately onto the necklace.
6. When finished, tie the ends together and let your child wear his creation.

For More Fun
Help your child make more necklaces to give out to friends, neighbors, or grandparents on Valentine's Day.

Personal Thoughts, Ideas, or Memories

How many hearts are on your necklace?
How many licorice pieces are on it?
What do you like best about Valentine's Day?

_____

_____

_____

_____

_____

_____

_____

_____

_____

_____

_____

_____

Fireworks Glitter

Your child will be dazzled by her own fireworks display.

You Will Need
- construction paper
- glue
- colorful glitter

Directions

1. Give your child a piece of construction paper.

2. Show her how to make thin lines of glue on the paper so that they resemble fireworks.

3. Let your child sprinkle colorful glitter on the glue.

4. Encourage her to experiment with one color at a time or with different colors on the same page.

5. Repeat as many times as you wish to make more fireworks.

6. When dry, display her fireworks on the wall.

Quick Tip
Shake off the excess glitter and save it for future art projects.

Personal Thoughts, Ideas, or Memories

How did you make your fireworks so colorful?
What do you like best about real fireworks?

_____

_____

_____

_____

_____

_____

_____

_____

_____

_____

_____

_____

Make a Mask

Watch how this mask gets your child into the act!

You Will Need
- scissors
- white paper plate
- glue
- craft stick
- markers or crayons
- assorted decorations

Directions
1. Cut out of a paper plate two oval holes for your child to peek through.

2. Glue a craft stick to the bottom of the plate for a handle.

3. Have your child decorate his mask with markers, crayons, glitter, stickers, etc.

4. Let your child wear his mask for a simple Halloween costume or just for fun.

Quick Tip
Your child will want to hide behind his mask again and again. Just remember to pretend you're surprised!

Personal Thoughts, Ideas, or Memories

What kind of mask did you make?
What do you like to do when
you're wearing a mask?

_____

_____

_____

_____

_____

_____

_____

_____

_____

_____

_____

_____

_____

A Handsome Wreath

This festive decoration makes a great holiday gift.

You Will Need

- pencil
- scissors
- white posterboard
- sponge
- red and green paint
- red construction paper
- glue

Directions

1. Draw and cut out of white posterboard a large circle.

2. Cut out the center so it looks like a large donut.

3. Sponge your child's hands with green paint and have her make handprints all over the wreath.

4. Wash the green paint off and sponge the tip of her thumb red.

5. Have her make thumbprints to look like red berries around the wreath.

6. When dry, add a red paper bow at the top and hang up for all to see.

For More Fun

This is a great activity for a holiday party with your child's friends!

Personal Thoughts, Ideas, or Memories

What did you do with your wreath?
What other holiday decorations
would you like to make?

_____

_____

_____

_____

_____

_____

_____

_____

_____

_____

_____

_____

Totline® PUBLICATIONS

Teacher Resources

ART SERIES
Ideas for successful art experiences.
Cooperative Art
Special Day Art
Outdoor Art

BEST OF TOTLINE® SERIES
Totline's best ideas.
Best of Totline Newsletter
Best of Totline Bear Hugs
Best of Totline Parent Flyers

BUSY BEES SERIES
Seasonal ideas for twos and threes.
Fall • Winter • Spring • Summer

CELEBRATIONS SERIES
Early learning through celebrations.
Small World Celebrations
Special Day Celebrations
Great Big Holiday Celebrations
Celebrating Likes and Differences

CIRCLE TIME SERIES
Put the spotlight on circle time!
Introducing Concepts at Circle Time
Music and Dramatics at Circle Time
Storytime Ideas for Circle Time

EMPOWERING KIDS SERIES
Positive solutions to behavior issues.
Can-Do Kids
Problem-Solving Kids

EXPLORING SERIES
Versatile, hands-on learning.
Exploring Sand • Exploring Water

FOUR SEASONS
Active learning through the year.
Art • Math • Movement • Science

JUST RIGHT PATTERNS
8-page, reproducible pattern folders.
Valentine's Day • St. Patrick's Day •
Easter • Halloween • Thanksgiving •
Hanukkah • Christmas • Kwanzaa •
Spring • Summer • Autumn •
Winter • Air Transportation • Land
Transportation • Service Vehicles
• Water Transportation • Train
• Desert Life • Farm Life • Forest
Life • Ocean Life • Wetland Life
• Zoo Life • Prehistoric Life

KINDERSTATION SERIES
Learning centers for kindergarten.
Calculation Station
Communication Station
Creation Station
Investigation Station

1•2•3 SERIES
Open-ended learning.
Art • Blocks • Games • Colors •
Puppets • Reading & Writing •
Math • Science • Shapes

1001 SERIES
Super reference books.
1001 Teaching Props
1001 Teaching Tips
1001 Rhymes & Fingerplays

PIGGYBACK® SONG BOOKS
New lyrics sung to favorite tunes!
Piggyback Songs
More Piggyback Songs
Piggyback Songs for Infants
and Toddlers
Holiday Piggyback Songs
Animal Piggyback Songs
Piggyback Songs for School
Piggyback Songs to Sign
Spanish Piggyback Songs
More Piggyback Songs for School

PROJECT BOOK SERIES
*Reproducible, cross-curricular project
books and project ideas.*
Start With Art
Start With Science

REPRODUCIBLE RHYMES
*Make-and-take-home books for
emergent readers.*
Alphabet Rhymes • Object Rhymes

SNACKS SERIES
Nutrition combines with learning.
Super Snacks • Healthy Snacks •
Teaching Snacks • Multicultural Snacks

TERRIFIC TIPS
Handy resources with valuable ideas.
Terrific Tips for Directors
Terrific Tips for Toddler Teachers
Terrific Tips for Preschool Teachers

THEME-A-SAURUS® SERIES
Classroom-tested, instant themes.
Theme-A-Saurus
Theme-A-Saurus II
Toddler Theme-A-Saurus
Alphabet Theme-A-Saurus
Nursery Rhyme Theme-A-Saurus
Storytime Theme-A-Saurus
Multisensory Theme-A-Saurus
Transportation Theme-A-Saurus
Field Trip Theme-A-Saurus

TODDLER RESOURCES
Great for working with 18 mos–3 yrs.
Playtime Props for Toddlers
Toddler Art

Parent Resources

A YEAR OF FUN SERIES
Age-specific books for parenting.
Just for Babies • Just for Ones •
Just for Twos • Just for Threes •
Just for Fours • Just for Fives

LEARN WITH PIGGYBACK® SONGS
*Captivating music with
age-appropriate themes.*
Songs & Games for…
Babies • Toddlers • Threes • Fours
Sing a Song of…
Letters • Animals • Colors • Holidays
• Me • Nature • Numbers

LEARN WITH STICKERS
*Beginning workbook and first reader
with 100-plus stickers.*
Balloons • Birds • Bows • Bugs •
Butterflies • Buttons • Eggs • Flags •
Flowers • Hearts • Leaves • Mittens

MY FIRST COLORING BOOK
*White illustrations on black back-
grounds—perfect for toddlers!*
All About Colors
All About Numbers
Under the Sea
Over and Under
Party Animals
Tops and Bottoms

PLAY AND LEARN
Activities for learning through play.
Blocks • Instruments • Kitchen
Gadgets • Paper • Puppets • Puzzles

RAINY DAY FUN
*This activity book for parent-child fun
keeps minds active on rainy days!*

RHYME & REASON STICKER WORKBOOKS
*Sticker fun to boost
language development and
thinking skills.*
Up in Space
All About Weather
At the Zoo
On the Farm
Things That Go
Under the Sea

SEEDS FOR SUCCESS
*Ideas to help children develop
essential life skills for future success.*
Growing Creative Kids
Growing Happy Kids
Growing Responsible Kids
Growing Thinking Kids

THEME CALENDARS
Activities for every day.
Toddler Theme Calendar
Preschool Theme Calendar
Kindergarten Theme Calendar

TIME TO LEARN
Ideas for hands-on learning.
Colors • Letters • Measuring •
Numbers • Science • Shapes •
Matching and Sorting • New Words
• Cutting and Pasting •
Drawing and Writing • Listening •
Taking Care of Myself

Posters
Celebrating Childhood Posters
Reminder Posters

Puppet Pals
Instant puppets!
Children's Favorites • The Three Bears
• Nursery Rhymes • Old MacDonald
• More Nursery Rhymes • Three
Little Pigs • Three Billy Goats Gruff •
Little Red Riding Hood

Manipulatives
CIRCLE PUZZLES
African Adventure Puzzle

LITTLE BUILDER STACKING CARDS
Castle • The Three Little Pigs

Tot-Mobiles
*Each set includes four punch-out,
easy-to-assemble mobiles.*
Animals & Toys
Beginning Concepts
Four Seasons

Start right, start bright!

If you love Totline® books, you'll love

Subscribe today!
Call 1-800-421-5565

Totline® MAGAZINE

For Ages 2–5

Active Learning

Engage young children in hands-on learning that captivates their minds and imaginations.

Across the Curriculum

Each issue includes seasonal learning themes, open-ended art, songs and rhymes, language and science activities, healthy snack recipes, and more!

Proven ideas

We print ideas that work and time-tested tips submitted by professionals like yourself!

Especially for You

So you can do your job easier, we include reproducible parent pages, ready-made learning materials, special pull-outs, and ideas that are truly age-appropriate for preschoolers.

May/June 1999   Restaurants: A Giant Classroom Project $4.00

Totline
Active preschool learning at its best

The Fish Who Wished He Could Fly
by Jean Warren

Jump Into Spring
With Garden Games and Nature Crafts

Backyard Field Trips

Active preschool learning at its best!

SPECIAL! Group Subscription Rates Call for details!

Activity calendar in each issue!

May 1999